THE
UNITED
KINGDOM

ATLANTIC

OCEAN

ORKNEY

SHETLAND

OUTER HEBRIDES

INNER HEBRIDES

SCOTLAND

NORTH

SEA

• Aberdeen

Glasgow •

Edinburgh •

55°

Londonderry •

N. IRELAND

Belfast •

Newcastle upon Tyne •

Middlesbrough •

IRISH

SEA

IRELAND

• York

Preston •   Leeds •

Liverpool •   • Manchester

Nottingham •

ENGLAND

• Birmingham

WALES

LONDON

Swansea •

Cardiff •

• Bristol

0   100km

• Southampton

Plymouth •

ENGLISH CHANNEL

0°

FRANCE

The United Kingdom

David Flint

MACDONALD YOUNG BOOKS

First published in 1992 by Simon & Schuster Young Books

Reprinted in 1995 by Macdonald Young Books

First published in paperback in 1998 by Macdonald Young Books

Macdonald Young Books,
an imprint of Wayland Publishers Ltd
61 Western Road
Hove
East Sussex
BN3 1JD

Find Macdonald Young Books on the internet at:
http://www.myb.co.uk

Design	Roger Kohn
Editor	Penny Clarke
DTP editor	Helen Swansbourne
Picture research	Valerie Mulcahy
Illustration	Janos Marffy
	Coral Mula
Consultant	Robert G Ford, University of Birmingham
Commissioning editor	Debbie Fox

We are grateful to the following for permission to reproduce photographs:

Front Cover: Robert Harding Picture Library above, Tony
Stone Worldwide below; Allsport, page 22 *above* (Steve
Morton); Keith Cardwell/TRIP, page 19; J Allan Cash, page 30;
Central Office of Information, page 24; Eastbourne Tourism &
Leisure, page 17; Energy Technology Support Unit, page 42;
The Environmental Picture Library, page 39 (A Greig); Eye
Ubiquitous/TRIP, pages 8 and 31 (Chris Bland), 23 (Davey
Bold); Sally & Richard Greenhill, page 18; Robert Harding
Picture Library, page 22 *below*; The Image Bank, pages 33
(Jeff Smith), 36 (John Hill); Levy McCallum Advertising, page
41: Life File/TRIP, page 29 (Lee Nixon); Magnum, page 37 (Ian
Berry); Metropolitan Police, page 25; Network, page 20 above
(Matthews); Picturepoint, pages 16, 20 *below*, 32 *left* and *right*,
34; Q A Photos Ltd, page 9; Rex Features, pages 13 *above*
left, 13 below, 40; Tony Stone Worldwide, pages 10 (David H
Endershee), 13 above *right*, 15 *above* and *below*, 27 (Trevor
Wood), 29 (Phil Matt), 38/39 (Colin Prior); The Telegraph
Colour Library, pages 14, 26; Zefa, pages 11, 21.

Printed in Hong Kong by Wing King Tong Ltd.

A CIP catalogue record for this book is available from the British Library

ISBN: 07500 2606 5

CONTENTS

Words that are explained in the glossary are printed in
SMALL CAPITALS the first time they are mentioned in the text.

INTRODUCTION

The United Kingdom is made up of England, Wales, Scotland and Northern Ireland. The country has changed greatly in the last 20 years, and is continuing to change. Some of the main changes include:

● developments in the countryside, where some farmland is no longer being used to grow crops or graze animals. This unused land is being put to other uses, for example theme parks or riding stables.

● towns continue to grow and expand into surrounding areas of countryside.

● town centres are being knocked down and redeveloped.

● more people are leaving cities to live in villages in the countryside from where they commute to work.

● old industries like steel and ship-building are declining and are being replaced by new ones such as electronics and computer manufacture.

● new motorways are being built to relieve congestion on the roads but, as a result, valuable countryside is often lost.

● new sources of energy which do not pollute the environment, such as wind and wave power, are being developed.

● people are becoming more aware of the need to look after the environment and the number of schemes to recycle glass, textiles and paper is increasing.

● large, out-of town shopping centres are

becoming increasingly popular, but they take customers from traditional city-centre shops and rely on people reaching them by car.

● in general people are living longer thanks to medical advances. However this means many more facilities for the elderly will be needed in the future.

As the United Kingdom changes, it adapts to changes in the rest of the world. The UK depends on the rest of the world for imports of a wide range of goods from timber, coal and iron ore to cars, computers and television sets. The UK also depends on selling its exports to the rest of the world, especially its oil, its manufactured goods like cars, and its services like banking and insurance.

◀ **New developments, like the Canary Wharf project in London's Docklands, aim to improve run-down areas.**

▲ **The Channel Tunnel marks an important new link between the UK and the rest of Europe.**

THE UNITED KINGDOM AT A GLANCE 🇬🇧

● Area

UK	244,100	square kilometres
England	130,439	square kilometres
Scotland	78,772	square kilometres
Wales	20,768	square kilometres
N. Ireland	14,121	square kilometres

● Population (1991)

UK	57.4 million
England	47.8 million
Scotland	5.1 million
Wales	2.9 million
N. Ireland	1.6 million

● Population density: 235 per square kilometre (UK)

● Capital: London, population 6.7 million

● Other main cities: Birmingham 1 million
Glasgow 734,000
Leeds 712,000
Sheffield 526,000
Liverpool 463,000
Manchester 449,000
Edinburgh 439,000
Bristol 391,000
Cardiff 388,000
Belfast 374,000
Newcastle upon Tyne 278,000
Swansea 168,000

● Longest river: Thames, 450 kilometres

● Highest mountain: Ben Nevis, 1,344 metres

● Language: English

● Main religion: Christianity

● Currency: Pound sterling, written as £

● Economy: Highly industrialised

● Major resources: Coal, oil, natural gas

● Major products: Automobiles, machinery, chemicals

● Environmental problems: Some pollution of rivers and coasts, especially around the North Sea and the Irish Sea.

THE LANDSCAPE

The United Kingdom has a very varied landscape from mountains to moorlands, from deep valleys to steep cliffs. In general the older rocks, like granite and basalt, are igneous rocks. They were formed from hot molten material which flowed out from beneath the earth's crust. Igneous rocks are more resistant to erosion and stand out as highland areas. These highland areas are mostly in the northern and western regions like Wales, the Lake District and Scotland. Ice has worn away the land to create deep U-shaped valleys and long lakes. These upland areas usually have thin acid soils so they are covered by heather, moss or poor grassland. Only in the valleys which cut into the uplands is farming profitable.

In the south and east the younger, softer rocks have weathered to give a fertile soil and some of the country's best farmland. These areas are mainly composed of

◀ **The Lake District is a glaciated highland area.**

▲ **The west and north are higher than the south or east.**

sedimentary rocks, like sandstone and gritstone, which were formed when sand, mud, grit or other eroded material was then compressed into rocks. The higher ground of the chalk hills of the Cotswolds or Chilterns interrupt such areas.

A third type of rock, metamorphic rock, is found in such areas as southern Scotland and the coast of Northern Ireland. Slate, and other metamorphic rocks, were originally igneous or sedimentary rocks but were later changed by heat and pressure.

◀ *The Thames Barrier is an important defence against the flooding of London. When sea levels rise the gates are raised. Since its opening in 1987 the gates have, so far, not been needed.*

As the ice locked up in the ice caps of the North and South Poles melts so sea level rises. This rise in sea level has drowned valleys in Devon and Cornwall to create inlets called RIAS. In Scotland the rising sea level has created SEA-LOCHS and FIORDS.

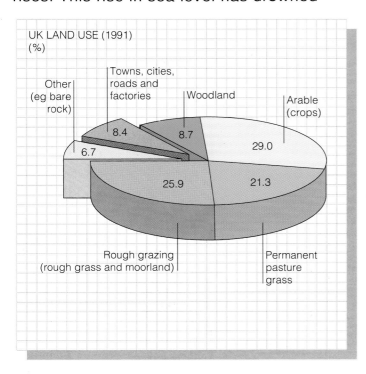

UK LAND USE (1991) (%)

- Other (eg bare rock) 6.7
- Towns, cities, roads and factories 8.4
- Woodland 8.7
- Arable (crops) 29.0
- Permanent pasture grass 21.3
- Rough grazing (rough grass and moorland) 25.9

KEY FACTS

● Nowhere in the UK is more than 100 kilometres from the sea.
● Cliffs south of Bridlington on the east coast of England are being eroded by the sea at the rate of 2 metres a year.
● The sea level around the UK has risen by a metre since 1900 and is still rising.
● Limestone rocks are quarried for use in making cement, aspirin, paper and chocolates!

CLIMATE AND WEATHER

The United Kingdom has a *variable climate*, which means that the weather changes rapidly from day to day. At the same time it is an *equable climate* which means that usually there are no long periods of very hot or very cold or very wet or very dry weather. However these *average* conditions conceal great differences between the different parts of the UK. Northern and western areas tend to be warmer and wetter in winter than the south and east. However in summer the south and east tend to be hotter, drier and sunnier than the north and west.

Weather can cause problems, especially during periods of fog, which may delay people travelling by road or air. Many motorway pile-ups occur during fog, and despite having automatic landing systems many planes are diverted to other airports during fog.

Sometimes fog becomes smog. This happens when smoke, dirt and other pollutants in the air become mixed with fog. Then air quality is very poor and can even cause breathing problems for some people.

Frost may cause difficulties particularly if it comes towards the end of spring. If it does, it can kill the blossom on fruit trees. Drivers, too, may be caught unawares by the frosty, slippery roads if the weather had previously been warm and spring-like.

Drought has been a problem in recent years, especially 1976, 1984, 1989, 1990 and 1991. Long periods with little or no rainfall cause reservoir levels to fall. The use of hosepipes is banned and people are urged to save and re-use water.

▼ *In January eastern areas are colder than the west. In July the south is warmer than Scotland and the north.*

▼ *The heaviest rain falls in the north and west of the UK, especially Wales, the Lake District, the Pennines and Scotland.*

July temperatures
January temperatures

Under 750mm
750–1,250mm
Over 1,250mm

0   100km

▲Sometimes very high winds cause severe damage to homes and property. This damage was caused by the great gale across southern England in October 1987.

▶Hot, sunny summers are good for business at UK resorts like Ventnor in the Isle of Wight.

KEY FACTS

● Since climatic records were first kept in the UK in the 1850s, the air temperature has risen by 0.5°C.

● The four warmest years on record were: 1987, 1988, 1990 and 1991.

● If air temperatures continue to rise, the polar ice caps will melt, sea levels will rise by 1.5 metres by 2020, flooding much of southeast England and East Anglia.

● For every 1°C rise in air temperature the death rate falls by 2.5% because people eat less food and suffer fewer heart attacks.

▼London, January 1991, and a traditional form of transport comes to the rescue of a modern one!

⚒ NATURAL RESOURCES

The United Kingdom is still rich in natural resources despite the rapid growth of industry in the last 250 years. Coal was the basis of the 19th-century Industrial Revolution. Large industrial cities soon grew up on coalfields in South Wales, the Midlands, Lancashire, Yorkshire, Scotland and North-East England. Despite such a long history of mining the UK still has enough coal for the next 200 years. However this coal will be expensive to mine and contains high levels of sulphur. When this coal is burnt it produces sulphur dioxide which is one of the main causes of acid rain. In future coal mined in the UK will have to compete with cheap coal imported from Poland, China, South Africa and the USA.

Oil and natural gas were discovered under the North Sea in the 1960s. Since then they have become very important sources of power. Recently new power stations have been built to burn natural gas rather than coal. However no-one knows how long the North Sea deposits of oil and gas will last. So the search for new deposits continues in the sea between Scotland and Northern Ireland.

Nuclear power has proved to be a very expensive form of energy. Surprisingly, the main costs are not in building nuclear power stations but from the difficulty and danger of dismantling a nuclear power station at the end of its life. In fact, electricity generated by nuclear power stations is almost twice as expensive as electricity from coal burning

KEY FACTS

● Oil provides 43% of the UK's energy, coal 33%, natural gas 18%, nuclear power 5% and hydro-electricity and other minor sources 1%.
● In 1979 the UK produced 122.4 million tonnes of coal. In 1991 the figure had dropped to 89.7 million tonnes.
● In 1979 187,000 miners worked in UK pits. In 1991 there were 58,000.
● Over 20 million tonnes of organic waste are thrown away each year in the UK. This could be used to produce methane gas.

◀ *The nuclear power station at Sizewell, Suffolk, is one of the Pressurised Water Reactors, or PWRs for short.*

▶ *This North Sea oil rig, with its support vessel nearby, is extracting oil and natural gas – vital UK natural resources. There are over 30 oil and gas rigs in the UK part of the North Sea.*

power stations and three times as expensive as that from natural gas burning power stations. Because of this it seems very unlikely that new nuclear power stations will be built in the UK.

Hydro-electricity is power generated by running water. It is important in remote parts of Scotland and Wales but is too expensive to transmit to the Midlands and south-east England where most people live. The estuaries of the rivers Severn and Mersey could be used to generate power from the rise and fall of the tides. However these projects would be very expensive and could harm sensitive environments such as wetlands.

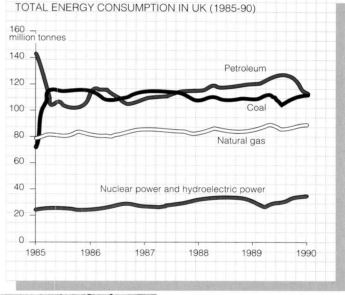

TOTAL ENERGY CONSUMPTION IN UK (1985-90)

◀ *Although the UK's coal industry is highly mechanised to help it compete with imports of cheaper foreign coal, the miners are as essential as ever.*

⚓ POPULATION

In 1801, at the time of the first census, the United Kingdom was a country in which most people lived in the countryside and worked on farms. There were a few large towns like Bristol and Edinburgh, but London was the only big city. Factories in 1801 were small, used little machinery and industries, such as weaving, were carried out in people's homes.

Things had changed greatly by the census of 1901. The Industrial Revolution transformed factories by using steam-powered machinery to do the work previously done by hand. Big new factories, with big new machines, grew up on the coalfields of Scotland, northern England and the Midlands. Cities like Manchester, Birmingham, Glasgow and Belfast grew rapidly as people flocked from the countryside to find work in the new factories. London continued to grow as a

major port and industrial centre, but the main area of population growth was in the Midlands and the north.

Since 1901 many of the heavy industries like coalmining, steel making and ship-building have declined. Many of the new industries like electronics have grown up in south-east England. Here they are closer to their markets in Europe and to the Channel Tunnel. So between 1951 and 1991 many

◀ **Commuters stream across London Bridge on their way to work. Many will have travelled a long way from their homes in the countryside.**

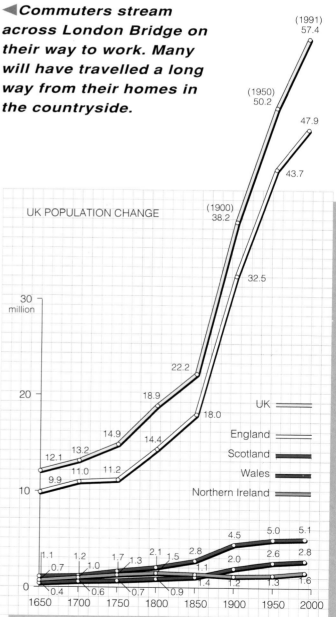

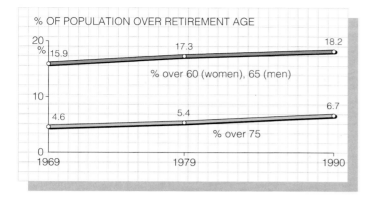

% OF POPULATION OVER RETIREMENT AGE

% over 60 (women), 65 (men)

15.9 — 17.3 — 18.2

% over 75

4.6 — 5.4 — 6.7

1969 — 1979 — 1990

people left the northern parts of the UK, where the number of new jobs was decreasing. They went to find work in the south and east, particularly in and around London.

Even in south-east England not all areas have increased their population. Slums and areas of poor housing in inner cities have been redeveloped. In the process people have moved away from city centres towards the edges of the built-up areas, where new housing developments have been concentrated.

SENIOR CITIZENS

Britain is a country with high medical standards, where most people have a balanced diet. One result of this is that more people are living longer. This increase in the numbers of older people has important implications for services like the health service and housing. In future the UK will need more retirement homes, old people's homes, and more sheltered housing projects to cater for the growing number of senior citizens. Similarly there may be a demand for more doctors, nurses and hospitals specialising in the care of older people.

▼ *Older people often move to places like Eastbourne because the mild, seaside climate helps their health.*

When people reach the age of retirement many decide to move home. Over two million people over 60 years old live at the seaside, in places like Southport, Eastbourne, Brighton and Bournemouth. They are attracted by the scenery, the weather and perhaps memories of holidays they spent in these places. The movement of retired people into these towns has led to a population increase in some of the main coastal areas of south and south-west England.

CITY VERSUS COUNTRY

However, other groups of people are on the move. In 1990 over 20 per cent of all COMMUTERS travelled over 40 kilometres to and from work every day. Despite the traffic jams and the extra time and travel costs they believe that the benefits of living in the country are worth it, because they have experienced living in cities. Of the 20

▲ *Providing services in rural areas is a problem because of long distances between places. Mobile shops are one solution.*

per cent of long-distance commuters, 17 per cent used to live in cities and made deliberate decisions to move out.

In contrast, many city areas are pleasanter to live in than they were even 50 years ago. The decline of heavy industries, the change from coal-burning steam engines on the railways to diesel engines and the passing of legislation to control the POLLUTION of the atmosphere has improved some inner city areas enormously.

ETHNIC GROUPS

The population of cities in the UK is made up of a large number of communities. All the people in these communities share the same basic needs: jobs, decent housing and a secure environment in which to live.

KEY FACTS

● The population of England and Wales grew by 0.5% between 1981 and 1991; in Northern Ireland it grew by 0.1% but in Scotland it fell by 0.1% in the same years.

● The Central Mosque in London has a congregation of 60,000, making it one of the largest in a non-Muslim country.

● 10% of the population of the UK move home each year.

● 40% of the UK's Afro-Caribbean and Asian population was born in the UK.

● The average life expectancy of women is 75 years and for men it is 71 years.

In the 1950s and 1960s people from the New Commonwealth (the West Indies, India, Pakistan and Bangladesh) were encouraged to come to live and work in the UK. There was a labour shortage and the UK needed all the workers it could get. Many of these New Commonwealth people went to cities like London and Birmingham where there were jobs. However, the newcomers often had to live in run-down parts of the cities, and many faced prejudice at work and in the community.

By 1992 the UK's 2.4 million Afro-Caribbean and Asian population make up 4 per cent of the UK's total.

▼ *Street markets still thrive in some towns and cities, particularly in poorer areas. Stalls are cheaper to run than shops, so market prices are lower.*

EDUCATION

All children must start school at five years of age and continue until they are 16. There are two systems of education. One is free and maintained by government funds. The other is private education which parents pay for. Confusingly, these schools are often called public schools. Up to the age of 5 children can attend nursery schools and kindergartens, if they are available in their area. From the ages of 5 to 11 children attend primary schools, although a few may go to middle schools when they are 9 and stay until 13. After they are 11 children go on to secondary schools, most of which are comprehensive, although there are also the selective, fee-paying public schools.

Children take GCSE examinations at 16 and some go on to take A levels or other qualifications at 18 or 19. Some students continue to universities or colleges of further or higher education. In Scotland there are no GCSE or A level exams. Instead, the exams are known as Highers.

LEISURE ACTIVITIES

People in the UK now enjoy more leisure time, and as a result membership of sports clubs has increased by 60 per cent in the last ten years. Some people prefer to spend their leisure time watching football or cricket matches, while others prefer more active pursuits, such as cycling, climbing, skiing and windsurfing. Angling is still the most popular participation sport. Leisure activities new to the UK, such as American football and baseball, are becoming popular.

Pressure on COUNTRY PARKS close to large towns is increasing, especially at weekends and bank holidays when thousands of visitors may flock to them to enjoy the

◀ *The UK has both state (above) and independent (left) schools. The funds to run state schools come from the taxes everyone pays. Independent schools get their money by charging fees. Both types of school try to provide a broad, balanced curriculum.*

KEY FACTS

● In 1991 98% of all households in the UK had a television, 55% had a video recorder and 20% a home computer.

● In 1991 4,241,000 children attended state primary schools and 3,551,000 state secondary schools. There were 641,000 children in independent primary and secondary (public) schools.

● The *Sun* is the best-selling UK newspaper. It is ready by 10.8 million people every day. Second is the *Daily Mirror* with 8.8 million readers.

● In contrast only 1.1 million people read *The Times* every day and 0.7 million read the *Financial Times*.

▼ *Regional celebrations are an important way of keeping local traditions alive. Here, at Luss, in Scotland, children take part in a Highland dancing competition, as their families have done for generations.*

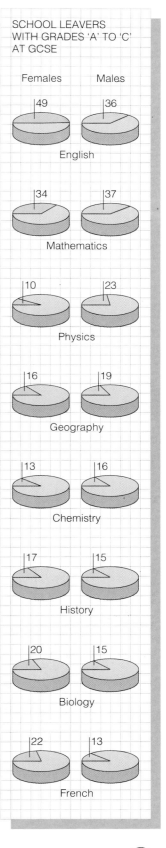

SCHOOL LEAVERS WITH GRADES 'A' TO 'C' AT GCSE

Females | Males

49 | 36
English

34 | 37
Mathematics

10 | 23
Physics

16 | 19
Geography

13 | 16
Chemistry

17 | 15
History

20 | 15
Biology

22 | 13
French

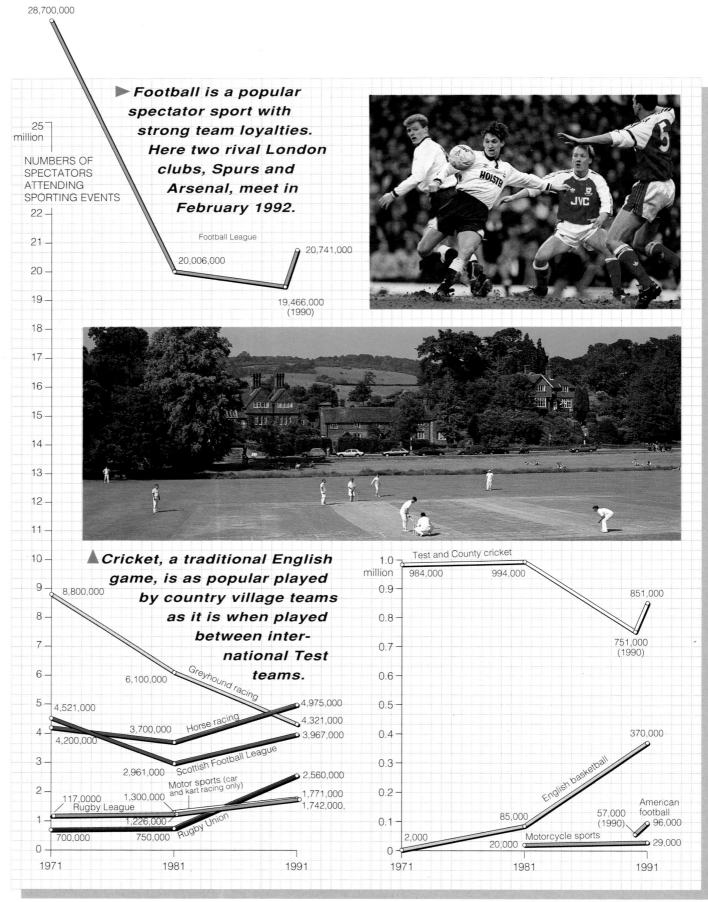

28,700,000

25 million

NUMBERS OF SPECTATORS ATTENDING SPORTING EVENTS

22

21

20

19

18

17

16

15

14

13

12

11

10

9

8

7

6

5

4

3

2

1

0

▶ Football is a popular spectator sport with strong team loyalties. Here two rival London clubs, Spurs and Arsenal, meet in February 1992.

Football League

20,006,000

20,741,000

19,466,000 (1990)

▲ Cricket, a traditional English game, is as popular played by country village teams as it is when played between inter-national Test teams.

8,800,000

6,100,000

Greyhound racing

4,975,000

4,521,000

4,321,000

Horse racing

3,700,000

3,967,000

4,200,000

Scottish Football League

2,961,000

2,560,000

Motor sports (car and kart racing only)

117,0000

1,300,000

1,771,000

1,742,000,

Rugby League

1,226,000

Rugby Union

700,000

750,000

1971

1981

1991

1.0 million

Test and County cricket

984,000

994,000

851,000

0.9

0.8

0.7

751,000 (1990)

0.6

0.5

0.4

370,000

0.3

English basketball

0.2

85,000

57,000 (1990)

American football

96,000

0.1

2,000

20,000

Motorcycle sports

29,000

0

1971

1981

1991

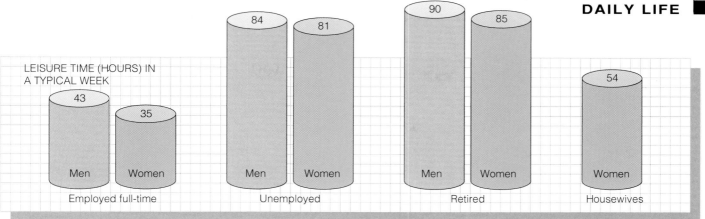

LEISURE TIME (HOURS) IN A TYPICAL WEEK

	Employed full-time		Unemployed		Retired		Housewives
	Men	Women	Men	Women	Men	Women	Women
	43	35	84	81	90	85	54

scenery. In the same way more and more people are visiting NATIONAL PARKS. For example, each year 14 million people visit the Lake District and 8 million visit the Yorkshire Dales national parks. This can cause overcrowding and congestion and damage the ENVIRONMENT people have come to enjoy.

THE MEDIA

Newspapers, magazines and books are important aspects of life in the UK. People in the UK read more newspapers than anywhere in the world, except the USA and Canada. There are over 120 daily and Sunday newspapers and no paper is directly owned by a political party. Recently the number of magazines sold has increased. This is partly because people have more leisure time and partly because there is a growing interest in leisure activities such as gardening, cooking, photography and DIY (Do-It-Yourself).

Radio listeners and television viewers have an increasing number of channels from which to choose. The British Broadcasting Corporation runs two television channels (BBC1 and BBC2), together with five national radio channels and many local radio stations. There are 14 independent TV channels.

▶ *The sales of regional newspapers like this one in north-east England have grown by 2% over the last five years. People still like to buy local papers to catch up with local issues.*

▲ *Each year the Queen, as sovereign and head of state, opens Parliament to symbolize the link between Crown and government.*

Britain's type of government is called a constitutional monarchy. This means that the sovereign (currently Queen Elizabeth II) is head of state but that political power is in the hands of Parliament. There are two Houses of Parliament. The House of Commons has 651 members who are elected by the voters for a maximum of five years. The House of Lords is made up of hereditary peers (whose titles are handed down from parent to child) and life peers (whose titles are given only for the peer's lifetime). The government is formed within the House of Commons from the political party which has a majority over all the other parties. The leader of this political party becomes Prime Minister who, in turn, appoints his/her cabinet, which supervises the day to day running of the country.

The main UK political groups are the Conservative, Labour and Liberal Democrat parties. There are also Scottish and Welsh Nationalist parties, together with the Democratic Unionist, Ulster Unionist, Social Democratic and Labour and Sinn Fein parties in Northern Ireland.

In England, Wales and Scotland there are three levels of local government: county or metropolitan councils, district councils and parish councils. Northern Ireland has one level of 26 district councils.

The services which we all need, wherever we live, are provided by different groups or organizations. Water and electricity, for example, are provided by specialist companies. Some are provided by local branches of the central government, such as the Department of Social Security which deals with pensions and other benefits. Other services, like education, are provided by the local authority. In some parts of the

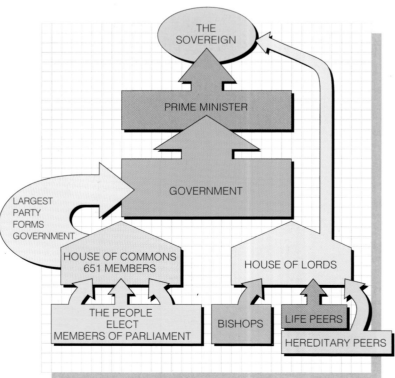

country refuse collection and street cleaning are also provided by the local authority, but in other parts private companies do the work for the authority.

▼ *There are strict laws in the UK about drinking and driving. At the scene of an accident the police use a breathalyser to check if the driver has too much alcohol in his bloodstream. There are now over 1000 more police officers in the UK than in 1983 and deaths from drink-driving have fallen by 10% in the same period.*

KEY FACTS

● Car crimes increased by over 50% between 1990 and 1991.
● The number of burglaries reported to the police increased by 20% between 1990 and 1991.
● In 1981 44,500 men were in UK jails. In 1990 there were 48,500.
● In 1981 there were 1400 women in prison in the UK. In 1990 there were 1800.

FOOD AND FARMING

Farming in the UK has changed a great deal in the last 30 years. In general farms have become larger, using more machines and chemicals but employing fewer workers. Some people now refer to UK farming as AGRIBUSINESS, that is an intensive form of agriculture which uses chemicals and machines to produce the maximum output of crops and animals at the lowest cost, which, in turn, means cheap food for consumers.

These changes in farming have had important effects on the countryside. Big machines like combine harvesters need big fields in which to operate. So hedgerows have been removed to create the larger fields. The hedgerows used to provide an important HABITAT for wildlife such as insects, birds and small mammals. Their numbers have fallen drastically as their habitat has been removed. Nitrogen from artificial fertilisers has found its way into supplies of drinking water where it causes serious pollution. Many insects, reptiles and birds have been killed by chemical pesticide sprays.

Loss of habitat is not confined to removing hedges. Wetlands are being drained endangering the common frog, newts and toads in some places. As people from towns and cities move into the country many buy up and convert old farm buildings into homes. These buildings were important nesting and roosting places for barn owls which are now also under threat.

Larger fields are more at risk from soil erosion, that is the removal of the top soil by wind or water. In areas like East Anglia great clouds of soil have been blown away

▼ *In areas of the UK, such as Wales, where the soil is too poor for cattle and crops, sheep farming is very important.*

KEY FACTS

● Over 8% of the population of the UK is now vegetarian and the number is increasing every year.

● In 1991 people spent £567 million on fish and chips, £291 million on burger meals and £261 million on chicken meals.

● In 1965 there were 210,000 farm workers in the UK. In 1991 the number had dropped to 102,000.

● Between 1945 and 1990 the UK lost 60% of its heathland, 90% of its natural ponds, 25% of its hedgerows and 80% of its ancient woodlands.

from the huge fields.

However farming is changing yet again. Some farmers have taken up ORGANIC FARMING using traditional fertilisers, like manure, and are replanting trees and hedgerows. As shoppers demand more organically-grown fruit, vegetables and meat so pressure on farmland has been reduced.

Farmers in Britain are deeply affected by the Common Agricultural Policy (CAP) of the European Community (EC). The aim of the policy is to give farmers all over the

Community a fair standard of living and to ensure that there is a reliable supply of food for everyone at reasonable prices. The policy works by setting a guaranteed minimum price for farm produce. This means farmers know they will be able to sell their goods and make a profit.

In the 1980s the EC wanted to encourage farmers to grow more cereals, such as wheat and maize, so high prices were set

▲*Oil seed rape is a popular crop, because the EC pay highly for it.*

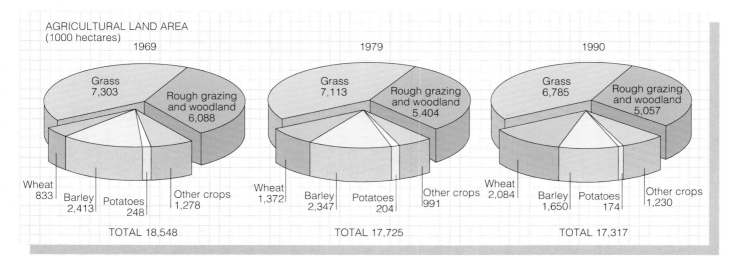

AGRICULTURAL LAND AREA
(1000 hectares)

1969
Grass 7,303
Rough grazing and woodland 6,088
Wheat 833
Barley 2,413
Potatoes 248
Other crops 1,278
TOTAL 18,548

1979
Grass 7,113
Rough grazing and woodland 5,404
Wheat 1,372
Barley 2,347
Potatoes 204
Other crops 991
TOTAL 17,725

1990
Grass 6,785
Rough grazing and woodland 5,057
Wheat 2,084
Barley 1,650
Potatoes 174
Other crops 1,230
TOTAL 17,317

▲*Intensive battery rearing of chickens is widespread in the UK. This method produces cheap meat and eggs, but is unnatural and stressful for the chickens.*

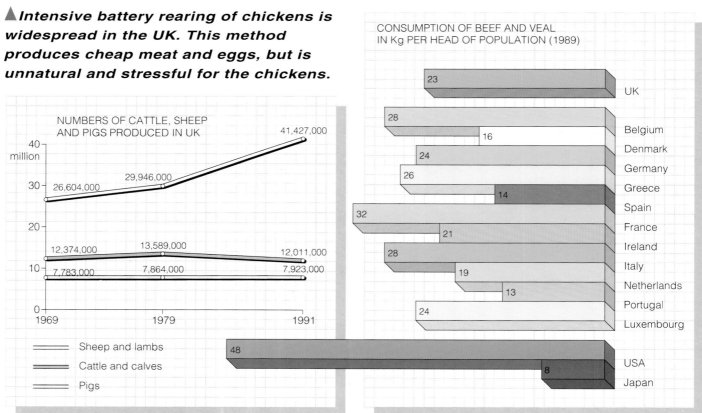

NUMBERS OF CATTLE, SHEEP AND PIGS PRODUCED IN UK

- 41,427,000
- 29,946,000
- 26,604,000
- 13,589,000
- 12,374,000
- 12,011,000
- 7,783,000
- 7,864,000
- 7,923,000

40 million
30
20
10
0

1969   1979   1991

——— Sheep and lambs
——— Cattle and calves
——— Pigs

CONSUMPTION OF BEEF AND VEAL
IN Kg PER HEAD OF POPULATION (1989)

Country	Kg
UK	23
Belgium	28
Denmark	16
Germany	24
Greece	26
Spain	14
France	32
Ireland	21
Italy	28
Netherlands	19
Portugal	13
Luxembourg	24
USA	48
Japan	8

for these crops. If farmers produced more than the EC needed the surplus was stored in warehouses. Exactly the same thing happened with beef, milk and wine. In order to reduce the surpluses the EC sometimes gives away products like butter, cheese and beef to pensioners and other needy groups. However the EC is now trying to cut down the surpluses by establishing an agreed maximum amount, or QUOTA, for the milk, beef, lamb and so on that each farm can produce. Another method of reducing surpluses is to lower the guaranteed price for crops like wheat and barley.

These changes in EC policy mean that British farmers, the most efficient in the EC, have had to adapt the crops they grow or the animals that they rear in order to stay in business.

The growth of country-wide supermarket

chains, as well as improved transport and refrigeration, has helped reduce the variety of regional foods. But the names of well-known foods and dishes give a hint of that variety: Cornish pasties, Lancashire hot-pot, Yorkshire pudding, haggis, Arbroath smokies, Welsh cakes, Bath buns, are just a few. Then, of course, there are cheeses. Stilton, Cheshire and Cheddar are known all round the world, but to get away from the dull, uniform varieties that used to be all the supermarkets stocked, smaller cheese makers have revived older, local varieties: Blue Vinney from Dorset, Cashel Blue from Ireland and the small round cheeses of Orkney, and there are many more.

▼ *In remote parts of Scotland farms, like this croft on the Isle of Skye, are abandoned as people move to towns.*

TRADE AND INDUSTRY

During the 19th century British industries like coal, steel, ship-building and engineering grew very rapidly. New mines, factories, roads, railways and ports grew up. Britain became the world's first industrial nation, exporting its goods all over the world. Areas like south Wales, the Midlands, Merseyside, Manchester, west Yorkshire, central Scotland, London and Newcastle became important industrial centres. The basis of all this growth was MANUFACTURING industry, that is industries which change raw materials like iron or wool into finished products.

However in the last 15 years these manufacturing industries have begun to decline. Factories have closed and people have lost their jobs. Industries like steel, ship-building, coalmining and engineering have been particularly hard hit. Many of these industries like car making have declined because of fierce competition from foreign companies. The textiles industry has also suffered because of competition from cheap imported goods. Other reasons for the decline of manufacturing industry include poor management, a failure to introduce new technology, a lack of investment and a lack of government support. This decline has hit the 19th-century industrial areas like south Wales,

▼ **Old industrial areas, like the Albert dock, Liverpool, are being redeveloped to revive the local economy and provide new jobs.**

◄Some of the most exciting modern architecture has been commissioned by industrial companies. This company headquarters and factory at Bristol is very different from the 19th-century industrial buildings (opposite).

the Midlands and central Scotland particularly hard. Empty, derelict factories and high rates of unemployment have created urban and social problems.

However some new industries, like micro-electronics, have grown up to replace the old ones. Britain is developing its high-technology (HIGH-TECH) industries making computers, electronics and telecommunications equipment. Most of these new, growth industries are located in a belt between London and Bristol, with smaller clusters in East Anglia and Scotland.

THE CAR INDUSTRY

The UK car industry has faced a great deal of competition from foreign imports since the 1970s. Foreign cars were cheaper and in some cases more reliable. The main problem was that in 1978 each Japanese car worker produced 30 cars per year, while the British car worker only produced seven.

During the 1980s UK car manufacturers

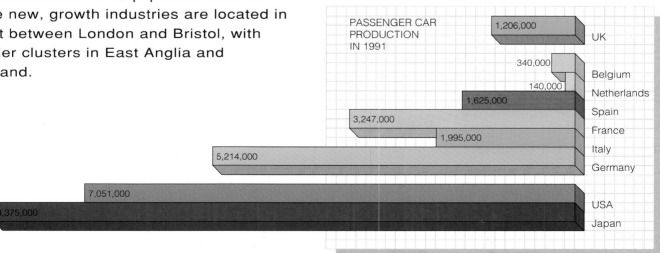

PASSENGER CAR PRODUCTION IN 1991

	Production
UK	1,206,000
Belgium	340,000
Netherlands	140,000
Spain	1,625,000
France	3,247,000
Italy	1,995,000
Germany	5,214,000
USA	7,051,000
Japan	8,375,000

Tourism is now a major industry in the UK, attracting visitors from all over the world. Two of the most popular attractions are Stratford-upon-Avon (left) with its associations with Shakespeare and Windsor Castle and the guards in their traditional uniforms (above).

fought back. They introduced new products and new technology, like automatic welding robots, on the assembly line. However some UK car makers were taken over by foreign companies. Hillman was taken over by Peugeot and General Motors took over Vauxhall. More and more car production is dominated by MULTINATIONAL companies, that is companies with their headquarters in one country and factories in many others. Now many UK car workers are employed by foreign-run companies such as Ford (USA), Peugeot/Talbot (France), Fiat (Italy) and

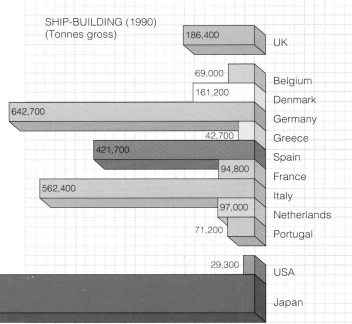

SHIP-BUILDING (1990)
(Tonnes gross)

Country	Tonnes gross
UK	186,400
Belgium	69,000
Denmark	161,200
Germany	642,700
Greece	42,700
Spain	421,700
France	94,800
Italy	562,400
Netherlands	97,000
Portugal	71,200
USA	29,300
Japan	3,251,100

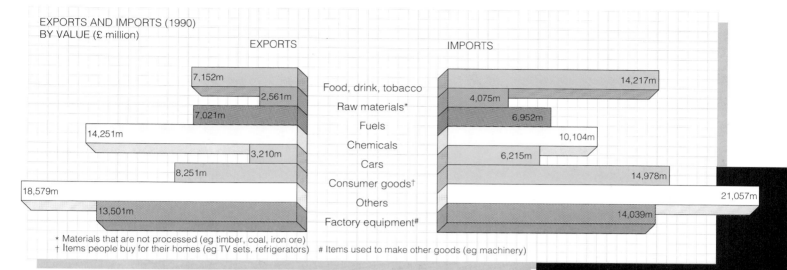

EXPORTS AND IMPORTS (1990)
BY VALUE (£ million)

	EXPORTS		IMPORTS
Food, drink, tobacco	7,152m / 2,561m		14,217m
Raw materials*	7,021m		4,075m
Fuels	14,251m		6,952m
Chemicals	3,210m		10,104m
Cars	8,251m		6,215m
Consumer goods†	18,579m		14,978m
Others	13,501m		21,057m
Factory equipment#			14,039m

* Materials that are not processed (eg timber, coal, iron ore)
† Items people buy for their homes (eg TV sets, refrigerators)   # Items used to make other goods (eg machinery)

Nissan and Toyota (Japanese).

The Nissan car factory at Washington New Town near Sunderland is an example of a factory built by a multinational company. Nissan wanted a base within the European Community from which to make cars for sale throughout Europe. The company was attracted to Sunderland by government grants and other financial help.

▼ *In the Stock Exchange's currency trading room dealers buy and sell the world's main currencies from dollars to yen.*

KEY FACTS

● In 1913 the UK built 59% of all the world's ships. By 1991 the figure was down to 2%.
● The Japanese government pays 38% of the cost of each ship built. In South Korea the figure is 40% but in the UK it is 21%.
● In 1972 76% of the 1.2 million new cars sold in the UK were made there. By 1990 only 37% of the 1.9 million new cars were UK made.
● The UK's pop music industry is a major 'export', worth over £500 million each year.
● The financial services sector (banking, insurance and the Stock Exchange) earned over £2.5 billion in exports in 1991

An important aspect of these multinational companies is that they are controlled from outside the UK. This means that decisions about factory closures or redundancies may be made thousands of miles away. However foreign-owned car companies are important sources of jobs and their expansion has provided work for over 10,000 people since 1989. By 1991 workers in Japanese-run car factories in the UK were producing 20 cars a year and the figure is still rising.

SERVICE INDUSTRIES

Although manufacturing industry has declined in the UK in the last ten years SERVICE INDUSTRIES like banking and insurance have grown. There are three main groups which make up service industries: transport, finance (including insurance, banking and property) and education, health and recreation. Service industries have become so important because they affect people in all aspects of their lives. Every time we visit a shop, make a telephone call, go to school, turn on water, gas or electricity or visit a bank or social security office we are using a service industry. Service industries, as the term suggests, provide services which people need.

Jobs in service industries are not spread evenly across the UK. Between 1979 and 1990 service industries grew by 7 per cent, which means 870,000 jobs. However 90 per

cent of these jobs were in only four areas: south-east England, East Anglia, the south-west and the Midlands. One of the fastest growing service industries has been business services, including advertising, market research, security and catering. Between 1985 and 1990 215,000 new jobs were created in this group of service industries alone. The hotel and catering group of service industries created another 120,000 new jobs between 1985 and 1990. The main groups of people who benefited from the growth of service industries were women, part-time workers and young people. As a result, all these new jobs were of little help to people who had been unemployed for a long time. Recently the expansion of service industries has slowed, but they have now become one of the most important sectors of industry in the UK.

ENCOURAGING INDUSTRIES AND EMPLOYMENT

In areas where unemployment is high the government is keen to encourage the growth of new industries which will provide more jobs. Areas with high unemployment may have other problems, such as many derelict factories and large areas of waste land. In some of these places the local councils have set up special ENTERPRISE ZONES to encourage firms to come to the area and so create jobs.

To encourage companies to come to the enterprise zones, the councils offer low rents and ten years in which the companies do not have to pay business rates. Planning procedures for factory and office developments in the enterprise zones are also made simpler and quicker, so it is easier for companies to get permission to set up their businesses. In this way, enterprise zones from Clydebank to Dudley in the West Midlands to London's Dockland have developed and grown.

Some cities, like Liverpool, have set up urban development corporations to redevelop run-down parts of the city to attract new industries. Urban development corporations are larger than enterprise zones and work by improving the local environment. For example, the development corporations demolish derelict factories, build new roads and even new factories. They cannot offer freedom from business rates, but they are able to obtain money from the government and private companies to improve the area and build new, modern factories.

◀ At Felixstowe docks, Suffolk, a ship is loaded with cargo containers. These are an efficient way of transporting imports and exports.

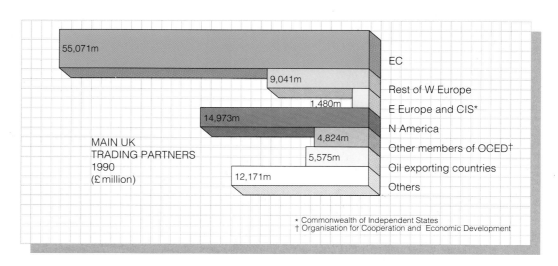

MAIN UK TRADING PARTNERS 1990 (£ million)

	£ million
EC	55,071m
Rest of W Europe	9,041m
E Europe and CIS*	1,480m
N America	14,973m
Other members of OCED†	4,824m
Oil exporting countries	5,575m
Others	12,171m

* Commonwealth of Independent States
† Organisation for Cooperation and Economic Development

An efficient transport system is vital for moving people and goods around the UK. Road transport has increased in importance during the last ten years, for both people and goods. Over 95 per cent of all goods moved in the UK now travel by road and by 1991 there were over 400,000 more cars on UK roads than in 1985. However this expansion of road transport has created severe traffic congestion in towns. Increased traffic means accidents are becoming more frequent and air pollution from vehicle exhausts has increased. New motorways have been built at the expense of areas of valuable countryside, and noise pollution has become more widespread. Attempts to solve these problems by introducing park and ride schemes, bus lanes or tidal flow schemes have been limited.

▲ *Commuters using the M4 face jams like this every morning and evening as they travel to and from London.*

British Rail has suffered from rising fuel costs, an ageing system of tracks which is expensive to maintain, competition from road haulage, low investment and pressures from commuters in south-east England. To meet these challenges British Rail has introduced computer signalling, specialised traffic such as cement wagons, and freightliners, which take containers of internationally agreed standard sizes. Newer and faster train services have also been introduced and the Channel Tunnel is giving a boost to rail services, especially in the south-east.

Air transport continues to grow in

importance, especially for passengers. There are regular services between London and major UK cities like Glasgow and Belfast. London (Heathrow, Stanstead and Gatwick) plus Manchester, Glasgow and Birmingham have important international services. Apart from passengers, airlines carry perishable goods, such as flowers, and light, valuable goods such as watches or jewellery.

Little freight travels on the UK's rivers and canals, although the canals are becoming increasingly important centres of tourism.

Because the UK is an island, freight transport by sea is important. The use of containers in which goods are packed at factories has speeded up the loading and unloading of cargo at ports like Tilbury, Harwich, Felixstowe and Southampton. The Channel Tunnel may reduce the number of passengers using cross-Channel ferries and ports like Dover, which had 7.2 million passengers in 1991, but the ferries are likely to remain important for the forseeable future.

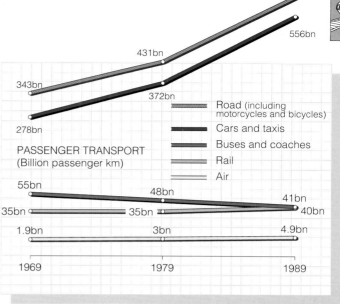

PASSENGER TRANSPORT
(Billion passenger km)

- Road (including motorcycles and bicycles)
- Cars and taxis
- Buses and coaches
- Rail
- Air

609bn
556bn
431bn
343bn
372bn
278bn

55bn
48bn
41bn
35bn · 35bn · 40bn
1.9bn · 3bn · 4.9bn

1969 · 1979 · 1989

KEY FACTS

● 22% of all the energy used in the UK each year is taken up by transport.
● 99.3% of the energy used by UK transport is in the form of oil.
● In 1970 34% of people travelled to work by bus. By 1991 the figure was only 25%.
● In 1970 43% of people travelled to work by car. By 1991 the figure was 62%.

◄ New types of transport, like the Docklands Light Railway (left) and the new Manchester 'tramway' system help to get people to and from work quickly without polluting the environment.

THE ENVIRONMENT

There is serious concern in the UK about the quality of the environment. People agree on the need to ensure that the environment is improved to achieve a better future for the nation's children, but they disagree about the best way to do it. Some people argue that the pollution of rivers and seas is so serious that immediate action is needed. Factories still pollute rivers and seas with toxic chemicals, while untreated sewage from towns and cities is still pumped into the sea. Oil tankers sometimes pollute seas and rivers by discharging oil into the water. There are regulations to prevent these types of pollution but they are difficult to enforce. Other people are in favour of trying to persuade polluters not to make things worse, rather than fining them for doing so.

Air quality varies from place to place in the UK. In general the air quality in towns and cities is poor because of fumes from factories and from car exhausts. There are measures to reduce pollution by fitting catalytic converters to car exhausts and trying to persuade more people to use public transport. So far improvements have been slow.

Acid rain is a problem which also affects many European countries besides the UK.

▼ *The photo shows why Lochain na h'Achlaise and the Black Mount in Perthshire are protected as areas of outstanding natural beauty.*

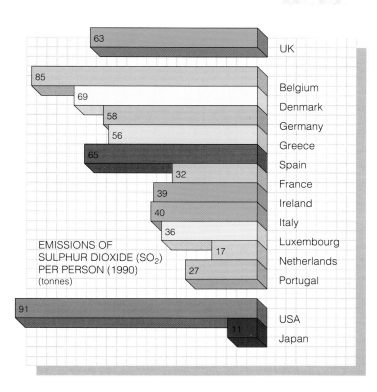

EMISSIONS OF
SULPHUR DIOXIDE (SO$_2$)
PER PERSON (1990)
(tonnes)

63	UK
85	Belgium
69	Denmark
58	Germany
56	Greece
65	Spain
32	France
39	Ireland
40	Italy
36	Luxembourg
17	Netherlands
27	Portugal
91	USA
11	Japan

▶ *Factory waste being discharged into the sea on Humberside. In the background is a chemical factory.*

▲ *People in the UK care about the environment and will object to developments they dislike. The protest here is against the Channel Tunnel.*

KEY FACTS

● 80% of lead in the UK is recycled.
● Northumbria has the least polluted rivers, followed by Wales. The Severn/Trent river system is the most polluted in the UK.
● 8.8 million tonnes of industrial waste were dumped in the North Sea in 1989. In 1991 the figure was 5.2 million tonnes.
● Despite attempts to clean up UK beaches, over 80% of all beaches fail to meet EC standards.
● Each person in the UK produced 355 kilos of waste in 1990. Each American produced 744 kilos. In Japan it was 344 kilos, in Germany 318 kilos and in France only 272 kilos.

Norway and Sweden get the sulphur dioxide which forms acid rain from power stations in the UK. The westerly winds blow the pollution from power stations in the UK and elsewhere in Europe across the whole of the continent. The acid rain kills trees, and even fish in lakes in Wales and Scotland. So there is great pressure on UK power stations to burn fuels, like natural gas, which are low in sulphur. It is also possible to fit special equipment in power stations which burn sulphur producing fuels, like coal, but the equipment is very expensive.

National parks, country parks and areas of outstanding natural beauty have been set up to preserve areas of particularly beautiful countryside. The aim is to restrict development in these areas so that future generations will be able to enjoy them, even if land in other areas is polluted by factories, farms or towns.

THE FUTURE

One way of thinking about the UK in the future is to consider how far present trends in industry, farming, leisure and so on are likely to continue. In the countryside people will probably continue to leave very remote areas, like parts of Scotland and Wales, where it is hard to earn a living. Providing services such as schools, hospitals and libraries is already a problem in some rural areas and this is likely to get worse.

Farming is already using less land, so the land which used to grow crops may in the future be used for golf courses or riding stables. More people will have more leisure time in the future, so even more visitors will flock to areas of beautiful countryside like national parks. Because so many different groups often want to use the same area of countryside conflicts will arise. There are already disputes in some places between, for example, hikers and motorcyclists, or horse riders and mountain bikers. In future planners will need to manage areas of countryside carefully in order to reduce these conflicts.

Sources of RENEWABLE ENERGY, which depend on wind, wave or tidal power, may, in the future, replace some of the coal, oil and natural gas used in the UK. However the search for new deposits of oil and gas will continue on both land and sea.

Water had been recognized as an

▼ *Princes Square, Glasgow, shows how shopping centres in the future may be enclosed, air-conditioned and centrally heated.*

increasingly important resource. A recent series of dry years has emphasized the problem, particularly in the southern and eastern parts of the UK, where the using of hosepipes to water gardens and wash cars has been banned. Scotland, Wales and north-west England get the heaviest rain – often over 1,000 millimetres a year. However, the biggest demand for water – for homes, factories and farms – is in East Anglia and the south-east. There are ambitious plans to move large volumes of water from lakes and reservoirs in the west, along rivers like the Thames and Severn, to the south. However, this would be very complicated and new canals would have to be dug to connect major rivers in order to get the water to the

KEY FACTS

● Geographers predict that growth and prosperity in the UK over the next 20 years will be concentrated in towns south of Oxford and east of Bristol. There will also be pockets of prosperity in other places, for example Edinburgh and parts of Devon and Cornwall.

● Government spending to support declining regions will be highest in Scotland, Wales and Northern Ireland. In 1990 the government spent £679 per person in Scotland, £722 in Wales and £1,270 in Northern Ireland.

● Inner city areas lost population at the rate of over 8% between 1981 and 1991, a trend that is likely to continue.

▼ *The power of the future? Salter's Duck is a way of harnessing the energy produced by waves. So far it is only experimental.*

places that need it most.

New industries, perhaps based in the countryside and using local skills to produce pottery, textiles, high fashion or even electronic goods, are likely to develop strongly. At the other end of the scale, multinational companies seem set to continue getting even larger, as they take over or amalgamate with other companies around the world. As a result even more office blocks will spring up in city centres, and more people will continue to leave towns and cities in search of a better QUALITY OF LIFE in the outer suburbs or in villages. From this it follows that the cost of travel in towns and cities is likely to keep rising. Sadly, pollution in both town and countryside will remain a problem.

FURTHER INFORMATION

The following organizations are all excellent sources of information about the areas and subjects with which they deal. Most can provide up-to-date booklets, maps and a host of statistics and other information.

THE ASSOCIATION OF AGRICULTURE
Farm Study Scheme, Victoria Chambers,
16–20 Strutton Ground, London SW1P 2HP
BRITISH AIRPORTS AUTHORITY
2 Buckingham Gate, London SW1
BRITISH COAL
Hobart House, Grosvenor Place, London
SW1 7AE
BRITISH GAS
326 High Holborn, London WC1V 7PT
BRITISH RAIL
Euston Road, London NW1 1HT
BRITISH STEEL
151 Gower Street, London WC1E 6BB
COMMISSION OF THE EUROPEAN
COMMUNITIES
8 Storey's Gate, London SW1P 3AT
FORESTRY COMMISSION, 231
Corstorphine Road, Edinburgh EH12 7AT
FRIENDS OF THE EARTH
26-28 Underwood Street, London N1 7JQ

GREENPEACE
Canonbury Villas, London N1 2PN
NATIONAL FARMERS UNION
Agriculture House, 25 Knightsbridge,
London SW1T 7NJ
ROYAL TOWN PLANNING INSTITUTE
26 Portland Place, London W1N 4BE
TOWN AND COUNTRY PLANNING
ASSOCIATION
17 Carlton House Terrace, London
SW1Y 5AP
WORLDWIDE FUND FOR NATURE
Panda House, Wayside Park, Godalming,
Surrey GU7 1XR

The following books may be useful for further project work:

The British Isles, Neil Punnett and Peter Webber, Blackwell 1985 (age 11–14)
A Geography of Britain, Rex Beddis, Oxford University Press 1985 (age 11–14)
The British Isles (second edition), David Waugh, Nelson 1987 (age 14–16)
A Geography of Contemporary Britain, edited by Rex Walford, Longman 1988 (age 14–16)
British Issues in Geography, CD Flint and DC Flint, Collins 1989 (age 11–14)

GLOSSARY

AGRIBUSINESS
Modern, intensive farming which uses chemicals and machines to increase production.

COMMUTER
Person who travels some distance to and from work each day, from one area or district to another.

COUNTRY PARK
Area of countryside planned and organized for recreation.

ENTERPRISE ZONE
Particular areas in towns which receive special government help to create jobs and attract new industry.

ENVIRONMENT
All the things that surround us such as people, buildings, woods, rivers and lakes.

FIORD
A valley formed by a glacier and then flooded because of a rise in the sea level.

GROWTH INDUSTRIES
Industries which are expanding and becoming more important.

HABITAT
A suitable place for particular types of wildlife and plants to live.

HIGH-TECH
Industries which use the most up-to-date equipment such as robots to produce goods such as computers.

MULTINATIONAL
Large company with branches in many countries.

NATIONAL PARKS
Large, mainly rural, areas whose natural scenery and wildlife are protected for public enjoyment.

ORGANIC FARMING
A system of agriculture which uses no artificial pesticides or fertilisers.

POLLUTION
Harmful effect on the environment caused by human activity, eg noise, dirt.

QUALITY OF LIFE
Level of well-being of a community and the area in which the community lives.

QUOTA
Amount of goods allowed, eg the amount of milk which can be produced for sale by one farm.

RENEWABLE ENERGY
Energy produced from a source which will not run out, eg wind, water.

RIA
A river valley drowned by the sea due to a rise in the sea level.

SEA-LOCH
A lake which has been drowned by a rise in the sea level.

SERVICE INDUSTRY
Produces a service for the consumer, eg banking, health, transport.

INDEX

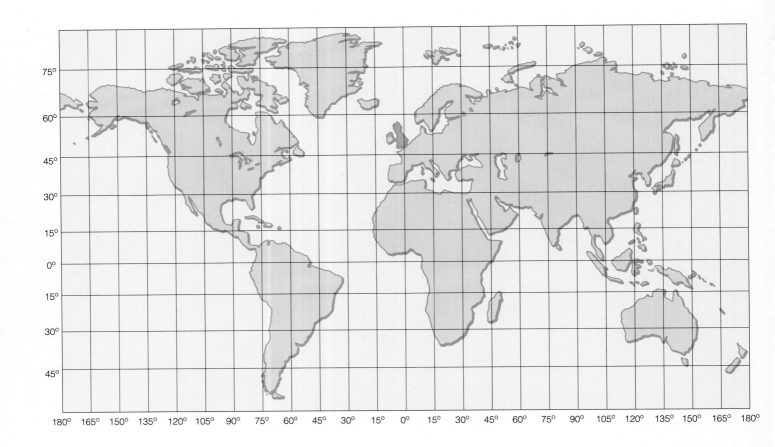